Pirates

© Aladdin Books Ltd 1995

Designed and produced by
Aladdin Books Ltd
28 Percy Street
London W1P 9FF

First published in the United States in 1995
by Copper Beech Books, an imprint of
The Millbrook Press
2 Old New Milford Road
Brookfield, Connecticut 06804

ISBN 1-56294-619-6 (lib.bdg.)
1-56294-637-4 (pbk.)

Design
David West Children's
Book Design

Designer
Flick Killerby

Editor
Jim Pipe

Picture Research
Brooks Krikler Picture Research

Illustrators
McRae Books, Florence, Italy

Printed in Belgium
CIP data is on file at the
Library of Congress

FACT *or* FICTION:

Pirates

Written by *Stewart Ross*
Illustrated by *McRae Books, Italy*

COPPER BEECH BOOKS
BROOKFIELD, CONNECTICUT

CONTENTS

INTRODUCTION

Pirates! What a host of images the word conjures up! Gnarled villains swigging rum beneath the skull and crossbones while terrified captives walk the plank and parrots squawk of buried treasure and revenge. Silly, hook-handed cartoon figures whose plans never go right and who cannot even defeat children, and handsome, heroic buccaneers plowing the seas in search of adventure and justice.

There is some truth in all these views, but they tell only half the story. There have always been pirates, from every seafaring nation, both men and women. They were not all terrible rogues, and they did not force their captives to walk the plank. Moreover, there are pirates today, robbing and murdering on the high seas.

The following pages explain all this, and more. They examine whether Blackbeard really was as evil as legend tells, and show how filmmakers and storytellers have mixed pirate fact and fiction in a way that must have Sir Francis Drake turning in his watery grave!

To find your way around this book, remember that it is arranged by area, i.e. Caribbean pirates are in one part, Mediterranean pirates are in another, and so on. Each part ends with a feature on a detail of pirate life; for example, the pirate schooner.

DANGEROUS SEAS

Pirates are the robbers of the sea. They have flourished whenever and wherever rich, defenseless merchant ships have sailed. The most famous pirate stories have been about cargoes of treasure, but in fact pirates have been eager to get their hands on anything of value, from gold bars to barrels of pepper and – nowadays – televisions.

Three factors make the perfect pirate hunting ground: a narrow, busy shipping channel; plenty of places for hiding, putting ashore for repairs, and unloading booty; and waters that are rarely patrolled by hostile navies. The well-known haunts (*right*) have been the Mediterranean, northern Europe, the Indian Ocean, the seas of the Far East, and, most famous of all, the Caribbean.

Caribbean The most famous pirate haunt of all. Spanish galleons filled with New World gold made easy targets for English privateers.

N. America

Atlantic Ocean

Pacific Ocean

S. America

S WASHBUCKLING HEROES! Pirates make wonderful subjects for films (*above*). Unfortunately, film-makers are usually more concerned with a good story than with telling the truth. Two of the early film stars who made pirate movies were Douglas Fairbanks Sr. and Errol Flynn (*right*). The pirates they portrayed had perfect white teeth, groomed hair and always acted like gentlemen – a far cry from the scurvy-ridden rogues you'll find in this book!

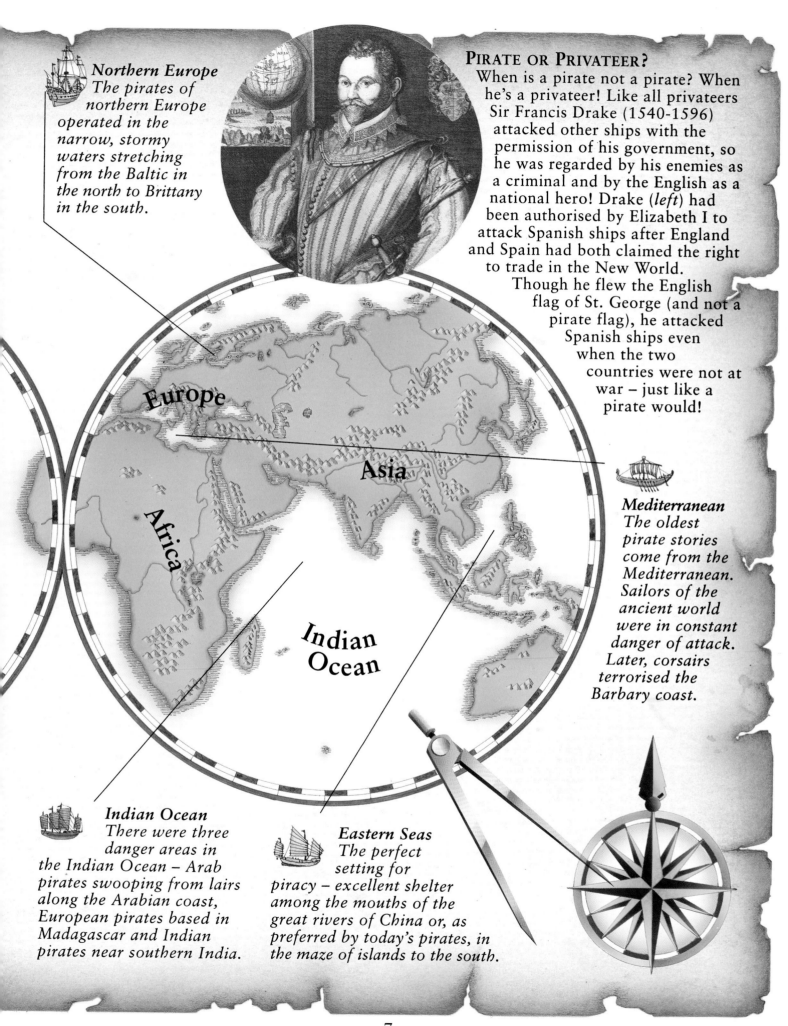

Northern Europe
The pirates of northern Europe operated in the narrow, stormy waters stretching from the Baltic in the north to Brittany in the south.

PIRATE OR PRIVATEER?

When is a pirate not a pirate? When he's a privateer! Like all privateers Sir Francis Drake (1540-1596) attacked other ships with the permission of his government, so he was regarded by his enemies as a criminal and by the English as a national hero! Drake (*left*) had been authorised by Elizabeth I to attack Spanish ships after England and Spain had both claimed the right to trade in the New World.

Though he flew the English flag of St. George (and not a pirate flag), he attacked Spanish ships even when the two countries were not at war – just like a pirate would!

Europe

Asia

Africa

Indian Ocean

Mediterranean
The oldest pirate stories come from the Mediterranean. Sailors of the ancient world were in constant danger of attack. Later, corsairs terrorised the Barbary coast.

Indian Ocean
There were three danger areas in the Indian Ocean – Arab pirates swooping from lairs along the Arabian coast, European pirates based in Madagascar and Indian pirates near southern India.

Eastern Seas
The perfect setting for piracy – excellent shelter among the mouths of the great rivers of China or, as preferred by today's pirates, in the maze of islands to the south.

PIRATES OF THE NORTH?

The pirates you see in films are elegant 18th-century buccaneers. Stripped to the waist under a hot tropical sun, they wouldn't have been seen dead in the icy waters of the Baltic Sea. Yet, despite the dangerous, rough seas of the region, pirates abounded in northern Europe. This was partly because, until the mid-17th century, there were no organized navies to root them out. Also, before the arrival of railways, sea transport was by far the quickest and easiest way of taking cargo long distance. The busiest trade route lay between the north (Britain, France, the Netherlands, Germany, and Scandinavia) and the Mediterranean lands. As coastal sailing ships navigated by hugging the coast, they could be easily attacked by pirate vessels lurking in the many river mouths along the route. Raiding parties also sailed up from the Mediterranean. These would land near a village, seize young girls and carry them off to be sold into slavery.

A LEAGUE AGAINST PIRACY

In the early Middle Ages the problem of pirates along the southern coast of the Baltic was out of control. Ship after ship was waylaid, its crew slaughtered, and its valuable cargo stolen. In response, a number of German merchants came together to form an anti-pirate league, known later as the Hanseatic League.

This league even developed its own type of ship, the *cog* (*right*). The cog's high sides, seaworthiness, and wooden castles at bow and stern made her able to beat off all but the most determined pirate attacks.

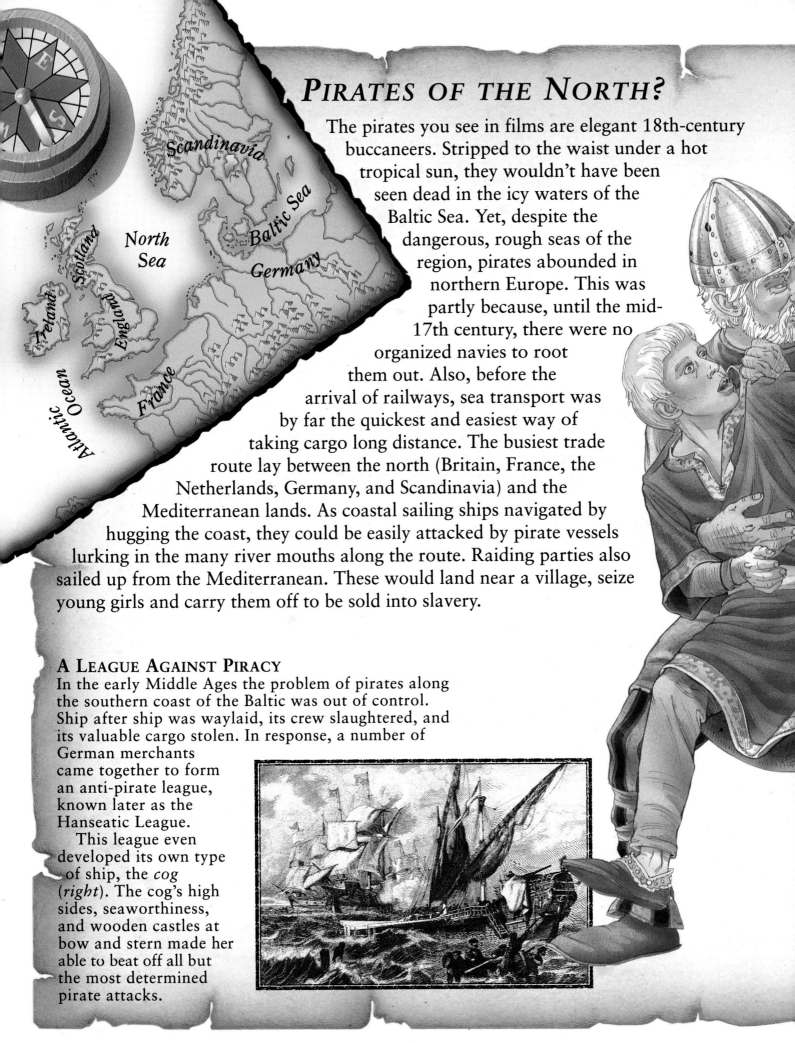

8

The viking longboat was designed for raiding (right). Her shallow draft let the Vikings row far inland and unload men and horses quickly.

Capture of Prince James
During the reign of Robert III of Scotland, real power rested with his brother, the ambitious Duke of Albany. Only the 12-year-old Prince James stood between Albany and the throne, so he was sent to France for his own safety. But in the Channel he was captured by English pirates and handed over to Henry IV of England. He remained a prisoner for 18 years.

THE VIKINGS – DARK AGE PIRATES

The Vikings were the most feared of medieval pirates. From the late 8th century these Scandinavian seafarers attacked not only the British Isles and France, but ventured into the Mediterranean and even across the Atlantic to America, which they called Vine-land.

They used classic pirate tactics – speed, terror, and surprise. Finding a suitable river, the Vikings sped deep inland. Ferocious carvings on their boats were an awesome sight to onlookers. As soon as they found a likely target, such as a monastery, they landed, took what they could, and were back in their boats before defending forces could be mobilized.

A PIRATE SINGSONG. A sure sign that the serious threat of piracy was over was the appearance of a comic operetta about them (*above*). In Gilbert and Sullivan's *The Pirates of Penzance* (1879) the pirates were sherry-drinking softies who refused to attack orphans, because they themselves were orphans. To their surprise (they were dumb as well as soft), every ship they captured appeared to be manned by orphans! In the end they surrendered to the police, and they turned out to be wayward noblemen who needed only to be loved.

The galleon has been caught alone and at anchor. If the ship was part of a convoy or under sail, the pirates would not risk an attack.

SPANISH MAIN, PIRATE HEAVEN

The Spanish Main was the name given to the New World territories seized by Spain in the 16th century. These stretched from northern California to the tip of South America. They contained the treasure of the Aztec and Inca peoples and the silver mines of Peru and Ecuador. Plundering this wealth, the Spanish began shipping it through the Caribbean and out across the Atlantic to Spain. The value of the cargoes exceeded men's wildest dreams – when Drake raided Nombre de Dios in 1572 he seized 15 tons of gold and thousands of silver dollars! Not surprisingly, the region was soon swarming with the likes of Henry Morgan (page 14), Blackbeard (page 16), and Mary Read (page 18).

Christopher Columbus
Christopher Columbus's (1451-1506, left) bravery and seamanship opened up the New World to Europe and with it treasures to be robbed.

Galleons
had two advantages: superior height and gunfire. To overcome these, the pirates attack from the stern (defended by only a few cannons).

The pirate ship, far smaller than the treasure galleon, has taken her prey by surprise. After drawing up alongside, the crew must make fast to their victim, lower the sails, and get aboard before the Spaniards can organize a defense party.

WILLIAM DAMPIER

William Dampier (1652 -1715, *right*) became a buccaneer because he thought it was the easiest way to travel the globe (which he did three times!) A scientist, he made careful observations throughout his travels, which he published in a book, *A New Voyage Round the World* (1697).

Native Americans *meet the Europeans who were soon to rob them of their gold and silver.*

HERNÁN CORTÉS (1485-1547)

Like Francis Drake, Cortés was an adventurer who hoped to make his fortune while fighting for his country. Born in Spain, in 1504 he ran away to Hispaniola. Having helped conquer Cuba for Spain, in 1519 he landed in Mexico with 600 volunteers and a handful of guns and horses.

Amazingly, within two years he had conquered the entire Aztec empire and had also beaten off a Spanish attempt to overthrow him.

LONG, THIN, AND DEADLY

Pirates armed themselves with whatever they laid their hands on. The one weapon they all carried was a knife. Most were short and sharp, and as useful for cutting rope as stabbing an opponent. The dirk (*left*) was designed just for fighting. Its long, thin blade could pierce a man's rib cage and enter his heart. Ouch!

BARBECUING BUCCANEERS!

While Elizabethan sea dogs such as Drake created havoc on the Spanish Main, a new threat appeared to Spanish shipping – the buccaneers. These men were not originally pirates at all, but Europeans who had settled illegally in the Caribbean. Here they learned from the native Arawaks how to barbecue their meat over a fire of green wood called a *boucan* in French (*left*). "Buccaneers" comes from this word. The settlers were forced from their farms by the Spaniards and moved to the island of Hispaniola. Once again the Spaniards interfered, clearing the island in the 1630s. It was not a wise move. Driven from their life as hunters, the buccaneers turned to piracy.

One buccaneer group based themselves in the Jamaican town of Port Royal (*below*). Jamaica had recently become a British possession and its governors turned a blind eye to the buccaneers' wild behaviour – as long as they accepted commissions to attack Spanish vessels. These "Brethren of the Coast", as they now called themselves, were a small navy for hire.

scale to read off degrees

micrometer for fine adjustments

CAPTAIN PUGWASH. Pure pirate fiction! Few make-believe pirates are further from the reality of vicious robbers than the jolly but bungling Captain Pugwash, master of the *Black Pig*. Part of his appeal is the fact that he is always rescued by his resourceful cabin boy, Tom!

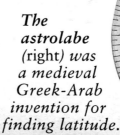

The astrolabe (right) was a medieval Greek-Arab invention for finding latitude.

NAVIGATION

Navigation means finding a path across the sea. Out of sight of land, this involves finding your position and plotting a course, for which you must know your latitude and longitude. Longitude, the east-west distance from Greenwich, London, could not be accurately measured until the chronometer's invention in the mid-18th century. Latitude, the north-south distance from the equator, was discovered by measuring the highest angle of the sun or the pole star above the horizon.

The Compass

The needle on a magnetic compass always points to the north. It can't tell you where you are, but lets you know in which direction you are going.

horizon glass

filters

How a Sextant Works

The sextant measured a ship's latitude with pinpoint accuracy. The navigator looked through his view finder at the horizon glass. This was half clear and half mirror. After lining up the clear half with the horizon, he adjusted the index mirror so that a known star (filters were needed if it was the sun) was reflected in the horizon glass (above). The angle of the star above the horizon was then shown on the angle scale below. From a set of tables the navigator could find out his precise latitude.

rays from star

image

horizon

index mirror

view finder

THE BUCCANEERS OF HISPANIOLA

The refugee community of Hispaniola was almost entirely made up of men. Most were farmers driven from their land by the Spanish, but they were joined by a motley crew of runaway slaves, deserters, and escaped criminals. They survived by catching wild pigs and operated in pairs, hunting and fighting together and leaving their belongings to each other when they died.

One buccaneer group, led by the French Protestant Jean le Vasseur, set up a fort on the rocky island of Tortuga, just off the coast of Hispaniola. It took hundreds of soldiers from five Spanish warships to finally drive them out.

coarse linen shirt

butcher's knives

hunting dog

rawhide britches

pigskin boots

SIR HENRY MORGAN

The most successful buccaneer of all, Sir Henry Morgan was part-rogue, part-hero. Born about 1635, he was kidnapped and taken to Barbados to work as a servant. He escaped and joined the buccaneers operating from Jamaica. By 1666 he commanded his own ship. Shortly afterward, the buccaneers elected him their "admiral." His first task, acting as a privateer on the authority of the governor of Jamaica, was to save the island from a Spanish invasion. This he managed in 1668 with a daring raid on Puerto Principe, Cuba, followed with a brutal raid on Portobello. He returned to Jamaica a hero, bearing a ransom of 100,000 pieces of eight. Two years later he was in Panama, raiding the coast and seizing Panama City. Although sent back to England to stand trial for piracy, Morgan was forgiven by King Charles II and even made a knight! Sir Henry returned to Jamaica as lieutenant-governor, where he died in 1688, having lived his final years in peace.

PIRATE FIREARMS

In the 17th century, firearms were heavy, inaccurate, and slow to use. But the 9-oz (250-g) shots they fired were devastating. A longer gun barrel meant greater accuracy, but the musketoon was still inaccurate over 35 ft (10 m).

Until the mid-17th century, most guns were fired with some sort of burning fuse. This made them dangerous on board ship, where fire was a continual problem. Keeping powder dry at sea was also difficult.

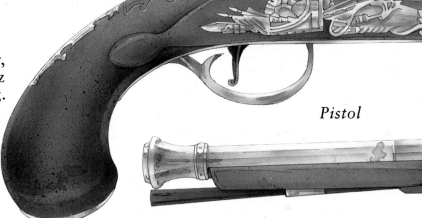

Pistol

Musketoon

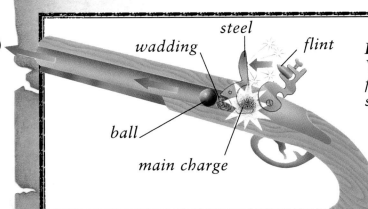

steel

wadding

flint

ball

main charge

Firing a Flintlock
When the trigger was released, the flint sprang forward against the steel, sending a shower of sparks onto the priming powder. This lit with a flash that passed through a tiny hole into the barrel and detonated the main charge. The force of the exploding charge forced the ball out of the barrel. Wadding kept the ball in place before firing.

The Seizure of Jamaica

The English took Jamaica from Spain almost by mistake. In 1654 an expedition left England led by Admiral William Penn and General Venables. Told by Oliver Cromwell (*left*) to seize Hispaniola from the Spanish, the expedition began disastrously.

In the attack on the Hispaniola port of Santo Domingo, the English forgot their water bottles, and Venables was so incompetent that he allowed himself to be ambushed twice in the same spot! Driven off Hispaniola, the motley force reached Jamaica in May 1655 and managed to land. After fierce fighting, the Spanish fled and the British claimed the island as theirs. Though captured by default, the island soon became a major base for raids on the Spanish.

Misfires: many things could go wrong with firearms – no spark, damp powder, trigger jamming – so misfires were frequent.

Morgan's Cunning Stunt

In 1669 Morgan was preparing to raid Maracaibo in Venezuela, when his flagship was accidentally blown up during a drinking bout. Nevertheless, he managed to force his way into the lake on which Maracaibo stood and entered the town. Then news came that the channel to the sea was blocked by three large Spanish warships. Undaunted, Morgan pretended to negotiate with the Spaniards while his men disguised one of their small vessels as a man-of-war. Fitting her with tree-trunk guns and cut-out wooden sailors (*above*), they launched her toward the Spanish ships. Too late the Spaniards realized it was a fire ship. Their largest vessel went up in flames and Morgan made his escape!

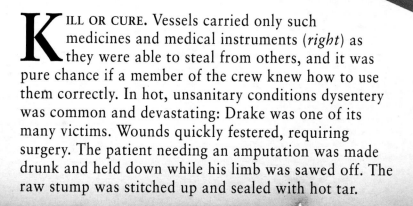

K**ILL OR CURE.** Vessels carried only such medicines and medical instruments (*right*) as they were able to steal from others, and it was pure chance if a member of the crew knew how to use them correctly. In hot, unsanitary conditions dysentery was common and devastating: Drake was one of its many victims. Wounds quickly festered, requiring surgery. The patient needing an amputation was made drunk and held down while his limb was sawed off. The raw stump was stitched up and sealed with hot tar.

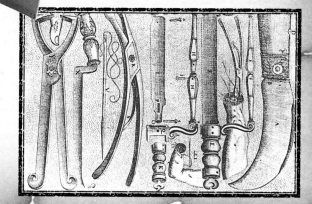

The Cutlass
The cutlass was a short, broad sword with a curved blade and one cutting edge. It was ideally suited to the cramped conditions on board ship where longer, stabbing swords would be difficult to handle. A single, well-aimed cutlass stroke could cut off a man's hand at the wrist.

Holy Smoke!
Blackbeard's terrifying appearance was increased by dense black smoke wafting about his head. It came from smoldering cannon fuses (page 14) stuffed under his hat.

BLACKBEARD

No one did more to create the image of a pirate as a murdering rogue than Edward Teach, popularly known as Blackbeard. A privateer who became an out-and-out pirate, Teach realized above all that terror was the pirate's chief weapon, so he deliberately made his appearance as terrifying as possible. Seeing him emerge out of a cloud of smoke, with braided beard and covered with weapons, his victims surrendered before a shot was fired. To make sure his captives knew what to expect, he cut the fingers off anyone who hesitated to give him their valuable rings (*below*).

Teach was just as tough with his crew, slaughtering one every now and again to remind them who was boss! His ship, the 40-gun *Queen Anne's Revenge*, terrorized the Caribbean from 1717-18. He beat off a British navy warship, captured four ships in Honduras and held the entire town of Charleston, South Carolina, to ransom.

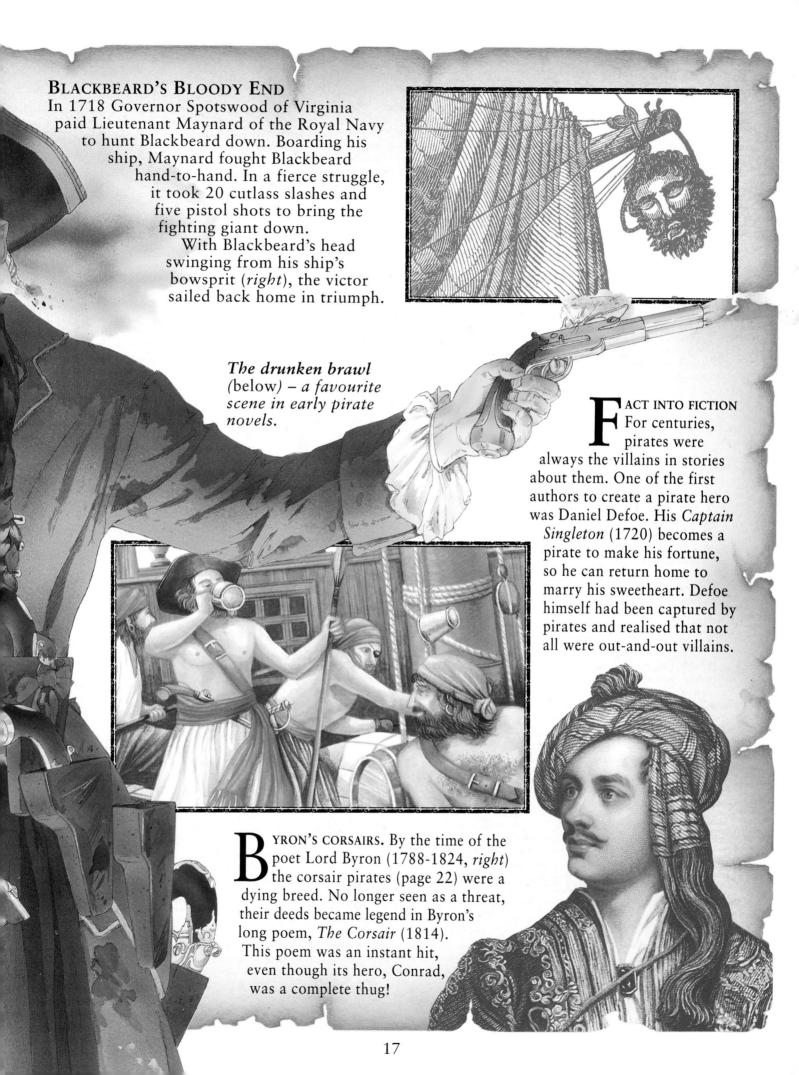

BLACKBEARD'S BLOODY END

In 1718 Governor Spotswood of Virginia paid Lieutenant Maynard of the Royal Navy to hunt Blackbeard down. Boarding his ship, Maynard fought Blackbeard hand-to-hand. In a fierce struggle, it took 20 cutlass slashes and five pistol shots to bring the fighting giant down.

With Blackbeard's head swinging from his ship's bowsprit (*right*), the victor sailed back home in triumph.

The drunken brawl (below) – a favourite scene in early pirate novels.

FACT INTO FICTION

For centuries, pirates were always the villains in stories about them. One of the first authors to create a pirate hero was Daniel Defoe. His *Captain Singleton* (1720) becomes a pirate to make his fortune, so he can return home to marry his sweetheart. Defoe himself had been captured by pirates and realised that not all were out-and-out villains.

BYRON'S CORSAIRS.

By the time of the poet Lord Byron (1788-1824, *right*) the corsair pirates (page 22) were a dying breed. No longer seen as a threat, their deeds became legend in Byron's long poem, *The Corsair* (1814). This poem was an instant hit, even though its hero, Conrad, was a complete thug!

BONNY AND READ

The world of the pirate was almost exclusively male. There were, however, a few remarkable exceptions, such as the Caribbean pirates Mary Read (*left*) and Anne Bonny. Mary's mother brought her up as a boy, and at fourteen she ran away to sea. After many adventures, including a short-lived marriage and a spell in the army, she went back to sea. She tried piracy, retired, then became a privateer. The life of Anne Bonny (*below*) was more straightforward. She married a sailor, but gave him up for the pirate "Calico Jack" Rackham. Based on Providence Island, the couple made a living by raiding Spanish ships in the Caribbean.

MANY PIRATE TALES come from two books: *The Buccaneers of America* (1678), whose author Alexander Exquemelin had actually been a pirate and seen with his own eyes some of the things he described; and *A General History of the Robberies and Murders of the Most Notorious Pirates* (1724) by Charles Johnson, which was based on interviews with real pirates.

Calico Jack's fame rests on his ferocity, his marriage to Anne Bonny, and his delight in brightly colored cotton (calico) clothes.

DOUBLE TROUBLE
For a time Anne Bonny and Mary Read joined forces. But in 1720 their ship was captured by the Royal Navy and the crew taken to Jamaica for trial. The case was clear-cut and Calico Jack and the male crew were hanged. As Mary and Anne were pregnant and the law did not allow the execution of women in that condition, their lives were saved. Mary soon died of fever in prison. Anne vanished without a trace.

Anne Bonny

Deadlier than the Male
Though few in number, there have always been female pirates – from Alwinda, who terrorized the Baltic in the Middle Ages, to the terrifying Ann Mills (right).
The 16th-century Irish pirate, Grace O'Malley, was known as "Grace of the Cropped Hair." O'Malley preyed on English shipping for 25 years until receiving a pardon from Elizabeth I in 1586. You can read about other women pirates on pages 42-44.

Mary Read

WIVES AND CABIN BOYS

Anne Bonny and Mary Read disguised themselves as men because there was no place for women on board a pirate ship, however tough they might have been. Some of the domestic work on board might be done by a cabin boy. These were unfortunate young lads, either captured or pressed into pirate service, whose job was to fetch and carry for the crew.

Many pirates had wives, but they left them ashore (*above*). Captain Kidd had a wife and daughters in New York. James Plantain, "King of Ranter Bay" on the island of St Mary's, kept a whole harem of women. He dressed them in fine clothes and jewels, but kept them far away from other men!

PIRATE LIFE

Pirates led two, or sometimes three, different lives. Many who went to sea to seek their fortune left wives and families at home. When they returned they lived as ordinary citizens. But once on board, they were seamen, keeping an eye open for likely victims and busying themselves with the ship's maintenance.

This meant cleaning weapons (rust was a continual problem with firearms), mending torn sails, swabbing the decks of salt and dirt, pumping out the bilges, and repairing broken ropes and spars. After a patrol, the pirates led yet another type of life (*above*). If they had been successful and had money in their pockets, they spent it on frantic sprees with wine and women. Drunken pirates were known to gamble away a fortune in a single evening!

Everyday items found in the sunken city of Port Royal

Clay pipe

Drinking bottle   **Pewter mug**

FOOD AND HEALTH

At sea life was very harsh. There was no way of preserving fresh food on board ship, so seamen either had to take live animals with them, or made do with dried food preserved with spices. Once they had been at sea for a week or so, they ate little but crackers and salt meat. For drink they had stale, slimy water and large swigs of rum or wine.

One of the major problems at sea was scurvy. This disease is caused by a lack of vitamin C (found in fresh fruit and vegetables). A scurvy victim's skin dried up, his gums swelled, his hair and teeth fell out and eventually he died. Citrus fruit prevents scurvy, but this was not widely recognized until the 18th century.

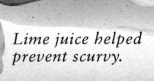

Lime juice helped prevent scurvy.

Who's for Captain?

Discipline on board a pirate ship was hard to maintain. Each captain had to run his ship as best he could. If he was successful, his crew might desert to return home with their loot, if not, he faced mutiny! (Left) Despite the job's danger, fights for the captaincy were common.

BELOW THE WATER LINE

A ship's hull soon became encrusted with barnacles and other marine life. This slowed the ship and made her difficult to handle. The only way to deal with the problem was to beach the vessel so she tipped over on her side, and scrape off the growth with sharp tools (*above*). This was known as "careening."

The rough underside of a ship gave rise to "keel hauling." A rope was attached to a victim's feet and hands, and unable to breathe, he was dragged around the sharp bottom of the boat. This torture was in fact used more by the British Navy than by pirates!

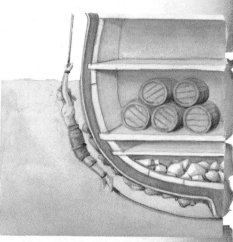

TREASURE ISLAND. Robert Louis Stevenson's *Treasure Island* is probably the best known of all pirate tales. Stevenson did his research well, which is why the book seems so realistic – he even used the names of real pirates. He drew on his experience of traveling by sea to make the voyage of the ship *Hispaniola* appear authentic. But above all it is the character of Long John Silver that has caught the popular imagination (*left*). As soon as we hear the word "pirate" we think of the one-legged rascal with a parrot on his shoulder!

PIRATES OF THE MEDITERRANEAN

In the Mediterranean, piracy was as old as civilization itself. However, the most famous age of piracy began with the Muslim conquest of North Africa in 709 A.D. The Mediterranean became a frontier between Christians and Muslims, and shipping from either side became a fair target. Christian privateers operated out of Marseilles, Malta, and Sicily. Their Muslim counterparts, known as corsairs, were based along what we call the Barbary Coast – the seaboard of Algiers, Tunis, and Tripoli. Unlike Caribbean pirates, the corsairs used galleys (page 26), and the most prized loot was not gold, but people. Captives were held for ransom, sold as slaves, or put to work as oarsmen.

The Bagnio (right)
The bagnio was the prison complex where the corsairs held their captives. It was like an enclosed town, with its own shops and taverns.
Prisoners faced a lifetime of hard labor unless they bribed a guard to let them work in the prison shops.

CAESAR AND THE PIRATES
Even the great Roman leader Julius Caesar (*left*) was once captured by pirates. Traveling slowly by boat to Rhodes in 78 B.C., he was seized and taken prisoner. Although well treated, he promised that once ransomed he would return and take his revenge.
In due course his ransom was paid and he was released. A few weeks later he was back with four ships and 500 men. The pirates who were not killed in his attack were crucified.

Bombardment of Algiers
When the Napoleonic Wars ended in 1815, the British and Dutch bombarded Algiers to end the threat from the Barbary Coast forever. As a result, 3,000 prisoners were freed.

Prisoners of the Corsairs
Once taken prisoner by the corsairs, European captives were chained and taken to the bagnio. If they were lucky, perhaps because their native country had a treaty with the corsairs, they would be ransomed. If not, they would either work for the master of the bagnio or be sold as slaves. An alternative was to adopt the Muslim religion, or "turn Turk." This might bring some freedom, but it led to problems if ever they met Christians.

THE BROTHERS BARBAROSSA

Christian-Muslim conflict in the Mediterranean entered a new phase with the expansion of the empire of Muslim Ottoman Turks. By 1500 they had occupied Constantinople (*left*) and carved out an empire along the eastern seaboard of the Mediterranean. Over the next century they expanded their control into the Balkans and along the north African coast.

Once again the ports of the Barbary Coast swarmed with pirates eager to prey on Christian shipping. Interestingly, the two sailors who did most to extend Muslim power over the sea were not Turks, but men of Greek birth. These were the brothers Aruj and Kheired-Din (*below right*). They were popularly known as Barbarossa, or Redbeard, from the color of their hair. Aruj joined forces with the King of Tunis and gathered a large fleet of galleys with which he took Algiers in 1516.

After Aruj's death in 1518, Kheired-Din became governor-general of Algiers under Sultan Selim I. From this base he spread Ottoman influence in a wide arc around the port. As well as taking other North African towns and capturing dozens of valuable merchant ships, he carried out daring raids along the northern shores of the Mediterranean.

SWALLOWS AND AMAZONS. The author Arthur Ransome used many of the fictional ideas about pirates in his popular stories for children (*above*). His heroes lived in a world that was half real and half fantasy, full of ideas from *Treasure Island*. Ransome's children fly the Jolly Roger from the mast of their dinghy and name their uncle after the famous pirate, Captain Flint.

The Jolly Roger
The name for the pirate flag, the Jolly Roger, probably comes from the French words jolie rouge, *which mean "lovely red". So early flags were perhaps not black but red.*

The skull and crossbones were a symbol of death, and like the red flag were a way of warning ships under attack not to resist.

Pirate captains made up their own designs (far right).

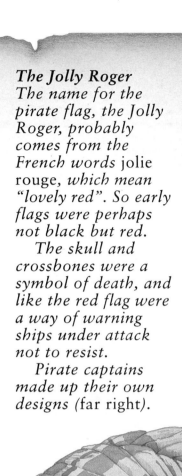

Calico Jack Rackham

Edward England

Thomas Tew

RENEGADE PIRATES
Several European pirates entered the service of Muslim masters. Some converted to Islam, others, such as Dutchman Simon Danziger, were allowed to remain Christian.

Western Europe was far in advance of the Ottoman world in matters such as chart drawing, navigation, casting guns and ship design. The Muslims tolerated the renegade pirates because they provided valuable technological skill and knowledge of European targets.

Blackbeard

Emmanuel Wynne

Christopher Condent

THE CORSAIR GALLEY

Developed specifically for use in the relatively calm waters of the Mediterranean, the galley was long and narrow, typically about 165 ft (50 m) long by 13 ft (4 m) wide. Powered by some 300 rowers, she could travel very fast for short periods or cruise under sail. However, the shape of the sail, together with the low prow and sides meant she was neither maneuverable nor very seaworthy. Nevertheless, in attack the ship was deadly. Much faster than a European sailing vessel, she charged the enemy at speed, homing in like a missile. Success depended on fixing the enemy with the ram before it turned away or the rowers became exhausted.

DRAGUT REIS

For five years Dragut Reis was the most feared of the corsairs. Like the buccaneer commander Sir Henry Morgan, he was more than just a pirate. He was a commander of skill and daring who led fleets into action.

Having been a slave on a Christian galley, Dragut Reis (*above*) knew his enemy well. However successful a corsair might be, his life was always in danger, and Dragut was eventually killed besieging Malta in 1565.

The Ram
A galley's tactic involved charging an enemy ship from the side, hitting her with the gigantic ram that rode up over the deck and made a bridge for corsairs to storm into the attack.

The Galley
Galleys had a high stern with a covered canopy to protect the rais *(the captain), a single mast with a rectangular sail, and banks of about 25 oars on each side.*

THE FIRST PIRATES

Cargo ships first sailed the waters of the Red Sea and east Mediterranean many thousands of years ago.

As these early ships were not very seaworthy, they kept close to the coast, making ideal targets for pirates who darted out from the shore.

ANCIENT GREEK PIRATES

During the Dark Ages of 1300-600 B.C., Greek cities surrounded themselves with gigantic stone walls.

For hundreds of years ferocious "sea-raiders" took over hitherto safe and busy sea lanes. But as Greek city states grew, the pirates were soon swept from the seas by the state navies' galleys (*left*).

Into Battle

Sea fights between Muslims and Christians were like land warfare on board ship. After the ram had stuck fast, fights were decided by hand-to-hand combat on the decks. The picture below shows Turks attacking Greek privateers.

GALLEY SLAVES

The life of a galley slave was about as unpleasant as one could imagine. Chained together on benches, six to an oar, they were kept alive with meager rations and rowed until they dropped.

Overseers walked between them, whipping them to work. If their ship caught fire or sank, unable to escape from their chains they were doomed to die in horrible torment.

Surprise, Speed, Terror

In most instances, a successful pirate attack depended on three factors – surprise, speed, and terror. Surprise could be achieved in a number of ways. The most common was to remain hidden in a creek or bay, then suddenly emerge into the path of an unsuspecting merchantman. Another tactic was to find a victim at anchor and creep up unawares to attack at dawn. Occasionally pirates achieved surprise by disguising their ship and crew, and revealing their true identity only when it was too late for their prey to escape. Speed meant catching the enemy as swiftly as possible, carrying out the attack and disappearing before help could arrive. Terror was achieved by reputation and appearance (looking as frightening as possible). Pirates often committed acts of terrorism not out of sheer bloodthirstiness but to build up a fearsome reputation. This made future victims less likely to resist.

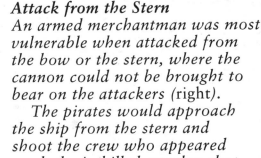

Attack from the Stern
An armed merchantman was most vulnerable when attacked from the bow or the stern, where the cannon could not be brought to bear on the attackers (right).

The pirates would approach the ship from the stern and shoot the crew who appeared on deck. A skilled attacker shot through the ropes controlling the sails, so the vessel could not get under way. They then jammed the rudder and clambered aboard to take their prize.

PIRATE CRUELTY. Not all pirates were cruel. Like keel hauling, the punishment of making a man walk the plank (*above*) over a shark-infested sea is largely myth. Nevertheless, piracy was a criminal activity and attracted its fair share of sadistic villains. There are stories, for example, of pirates setting fire to their victims, firing them from cannons, blinding them, cutting off their limbs, marooning them and worse. One pirate cut open his victims, tied one end of their intestine to the ground and made them dance to pull out the rest of their gut.

DISGUISE AND DECEPTION

Pirates used various tricks to catch a potential prize off-guard. One of the most obvious was to fly the flag of a friendly nation.

Other ploys were to hide the guns on a pirate ship and drag ropes behind it to slow it down – both helping to create the impression of a merchantman weighed down by cargo.

It was even rumoured that some crews dressed up as women (*right*). Since women were rarely carried on pirate vessels (see page 18), the prey relaxed in the mistaken belief that they were safe from attack.

AT THE SCAFFOLD

The penalty for a sailor convicted of piracy was death. In Muslim lands the sentence was carried out by beheading. In Britain and her colonies hanging was preferred (*left*).

Executions generally took place in Wapping, London and huge crowds stood along the river banks and on boats to get a good view of the scaffold. Here the pirate heard his last sermon, addressed the crowd and was duly executed. To show how the world had been cleansed of evil, his body was left swinging until washed by three tides. The head might be stuck on a pole as a warning to others (*right*).

Until the 18th century, it was rare for the whole crew to be hanged, as there was a shortage of good crews. Many claimed that they had been forced into piracy.

Pirates of the Indian Ocean

Being one of the great trade routes of the world, the Indian Ocean was bedeviled with pirates from earliest times. For centuries piracy was largely a local problem, affecting Arab and Indian merchants. However, in 1497-8 Vasco da Gama sailed around the Cape of Good Hope and reached India, pioneering the way east for European vessels. No sooner had ships from Portugal, Holland, France, and Britain begun to trade regularly with the East, than the Indian Ocean was alive with pirates of every nation. To begin with the Europeans preyed on local shipping. Before long, they turned to the great trading ships of the East India Company. In the mid-17th century, buccaneers like Henry Avery (*below*) arrived from the Caribbean (page 34). Though they were soon suppressed, the threat from native pirates remained until the mid-18th century (page 36).

The Gujarati Rovers

Before the arrival of European vessels, the most feared pirates in the Indian Ocean were the Gujarati Rovers. Taking their families with them, they patrolled the west coast of India during the summer months. Their boats spread out 6 miles (10 km) apart, forming a net through which only the most intrepid or fortunate merchantman could pass. They also forced prisoners to swallow tamarind root (*left*), causing them to vomit up any jewels swallowed for safekeeping!

THE WEALTH OF THE INDIES

The highly prized cargoes sought by pirates in the Indian Ocean were not gold and silver, but silks, jewels, ivory, and all types of spices (pepper, cinnamon, and nutmeg) needed to flavor and preserve food.

THE IMAGE OF THE PIRATE

The popular image of the pirate (*left*) is largely myth. Most real pirates were dirty, unshaven, with broken or missing teeth, bad skin and tattered, ill-fitting clothes. Few pirates, if any, wore earrings – they would only get caught in the rigging. And no true pirate dreamed of having a parrot on his shoulder. Not only would it have made a mess on his clothes, but he would have eaten it when supplies ran low!

The Dhow

The dhow was an Arab vessel which was also used by pirates in the eastern Mediterranean, the Red Sea, and the western Indian Ocean. Her principal features were her tapered shape at either end and the single triangular (lateen) sail (see center of main picture).

P for Pirate (and Painful!)

In 1683 the British Admiralty gave authority to the East India Company to deal with piracy as it thought fit.

Those not hanged were flogged unmercifully or branded with the letter P (above) on the forehead – or both!

MADAGASCAR, PIRATE KINGDOM

Madagascar and its surrounding islands were a unique pirate base. Here, for about 30 years, European buccaneers such as James Plantain ran their own pirate "kingdom." The remote and largely uninhabited tropical islands off the east coast of Africa provided excellent natural harbors. In its heyday, St. Mary's harbor sheltered more than a dozen pirate ships at the same time. When George Raynor returned here after seizing an Indian vessel in the Red Sea, he distributed loot worth £1,100 to every single member of his crew. It was sufficient to set them up for the rest of their lives. But this island existence was far from perfect. Too often it was not the pirates who made their fortunes, but the merchants who bought their booty for shipment to the West. There was little for the pirates to do but lie around, drinking and gambling (*right*). Not surprisingly, by about 1720 the "kingdom" had collapsed.

R EAL-LIFE ROBINSON. Daniel Defoe's story of *Robinson Crusoe* was based on the real-life adventure of Alexander Selkirk. In 1707 Selkirk was sailing with the pirate William Dampier. The two men did not get along. After an argument, Selkirk asked to be set ashore. Dampier duly obliged, leaving Selkirk on the uninhabited island of Juan Fernandez. As the pirates sailed off over the horizon, Selkirk changed his mind. Too late! It was four years before he was rescued.

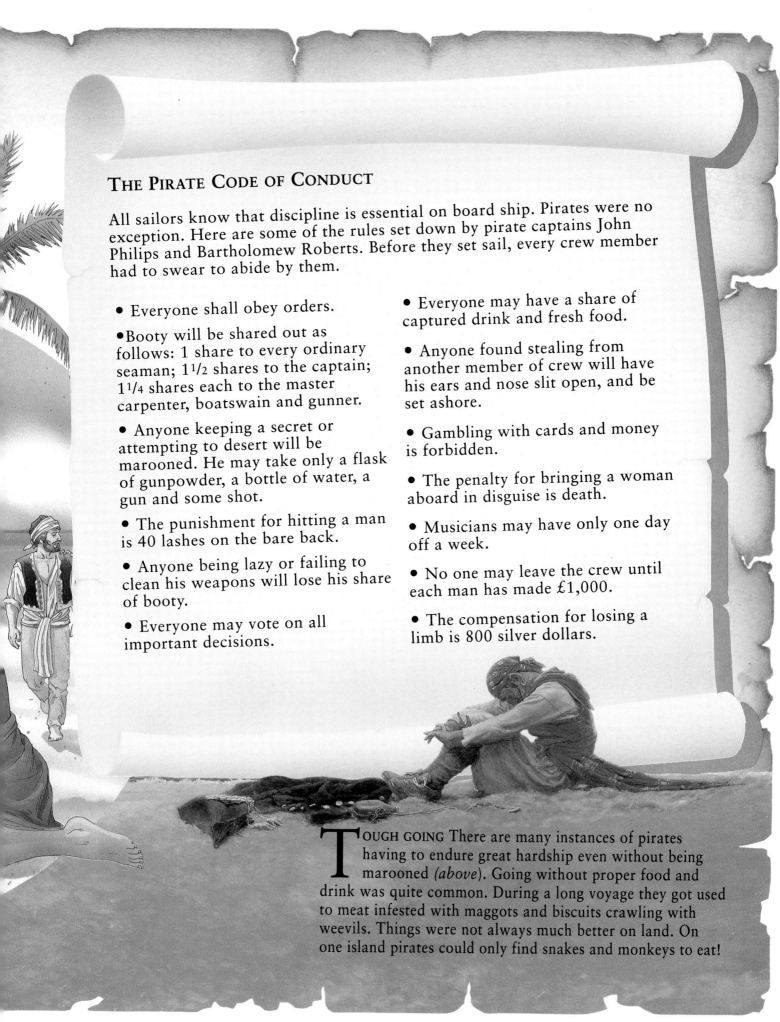

THE PIRATE CODE OF CONDUCT

All sailors know that discipline is essential on board ship. Pirates were no exception. Here are some of the rules set down by pirate captains John Philips and Bartholomew Roberts. Before they set sail, every crew member had to swear to abide by them.

- Everyone shall obey orders.

- Booty will be shared out as follows: 1 share to every ordinary seaman; 1½ shares to the captain; 1¼ shares each to the master carpenter, boatswain and gunner.

- Anyone keeping a secret or attempting to desert will be marooned. He may take only a flask of gunpowder, a bottle of water, a gun and some shot.

- The punishment for hitting a man is 40 lashes on the bare back.

- Anyone being lazy or failing to clean his weapons will lose his share of booty.

- Everyone may vote on all important decisions.

- Everyone may have a share of captured drink and fresh food.

- Anyone found stealing from another member of crew will have his ears and nose slit open, and be set ashore.

- Gambling with cards and money is forbidden.

- The penalty for bringing a woman aboard in disguise is death.

- Musicians may have only one day off a week.

- No one may leave the crew until each man has made £1,000.

- The compensation for losing a limb is 800 silver dollars.

TOUGH GOING There are many instances of pirates having to endure great hardship even without being marooned (*above*). Going without proper food and drink was quite common. During a long voyage they got used to meat infested with maggots and biscuits crawling with weevils. Things were not always much better on land. On one island pirates could only find snakes and monkeys to eat!

AVERY AND KIDD

Among the most famous pirates who stalked the Indian Ocean were Henry Avery and William Kidd. Avery (*left*) was a jolly sea captain who served in the Royal Navy before entering into Spanish pay as a privateer in 1694. He captured the British vessel *Charles II*, changed her name to the *Fancy,* and went off to Madagascar as a pirate. He soon had six ships under his command and took several prizes, ending in the capture of the *Gang-ir-Sawai* which earned him £325,000. Loaded with diamonds, he returned to England via the Caribbean – and vanished. Legend has it that he died in poverty after merchants swindled him out of his fortune. New York-based Kidd was a successful businessman who tried his hand at pirate hunting. But Kidd was no seaman, and losing his nerve, he killed a member of his crew and turned pirate himself. After seizing the *Quedah Merchant*, he returned to New York, hoping for a pardon.

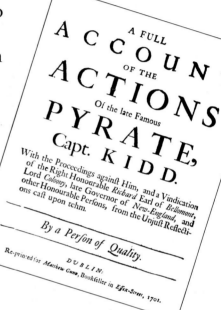

A FULL ACCOUNT OF THE ACTIONS Of the late Famous PYRATE, Capt. KIDD. With the Proceedings against Him, and a Vindication of the Right Honourable *Richard* Earl of *Bellomont,* Lord *Coloony,* late Governor of *New-England,* and other Honourable Persons, from the Unjust Reflections cast upon tchm.

By a Person of Quality.

DUBLIN: Re-printed for *Matthew Gunn,* Bookseller in *Essex-Street,* 1701.

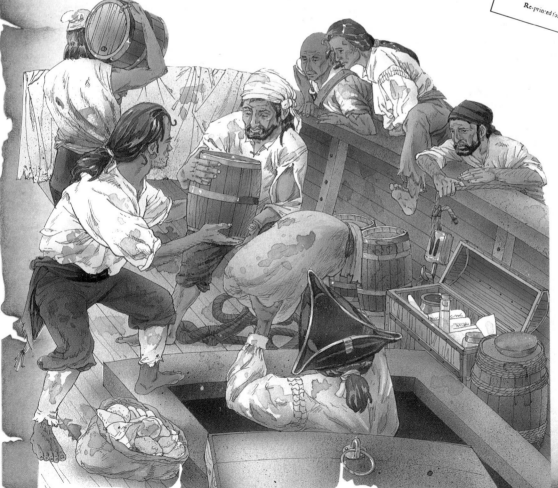

LOOT

"Pieces of eight, pieces of eight!" squawked Long John Silver's parrot. But money was not the only thing the pirates wanted. Just as important were the supplies required to keep their ship afloat and themselves alive (*left*). So pirates also carried off food, drink (especially rum, which lasted well in the tropical climate), rope, tools, anchors, medicines, tackle, and even masts and spars.

P ETER PAN, written by J. M. Barrie in 1904, is the perfect illustration of the progress of pirates from fact to fiction. The story takes place in Never-Never Land, peopled by lost children and fantasy figures from children's fiction – fairies, Indians, and pirates. Captain Hook (seen *below* fighting Peter Pan) is the ultimate fictional pirate, complete with a hook in place of a hand (cut off by Peter Pan) and pursued to his death by the crocodile that had eaten his severed fist. The piece earned undying popularity from the moment it was published and was successfully adapted for stage and screen.

A STICKY END

The men who had funded Kidd's privateering venture refused to stand by him when he returned to New York. He was sent to London for trial. The Admiralty found him guilty of murder and piracy, and sentenced him to be hanged at Execution Dock. Totally drunk on his day of execution he leaped about so much that the rope snapped and he fell into the mud below the scaffold. Officials hauled him out and strung him up again, this time successfully. After his death his body was coated with tar and placed in an iron cage. For years it hung there as a warning to other pirates.

THE MARATHA WARS

By 1720 the Indian Ocean was just about clear of European pirates. But a new threat to East-West trade had arisen – the sailors of the Maratha kingdoms of western India. The Maratha rulers, in particular Kanhoji Angria, controlled the entire seaboard from Bombay to Goa and claimed the right to tax ships passing along the coast.

The British East India Company rejected this claim. The Angrians constructed a fleet of speedy vessels named "grabs" and defended their shores with a string of huge forts. Though a peace treaty was signed in 1713, fighting soon broke out again. The British tried in vain to break Angrian power. They even built a massive floating battery with which to pound the Indian forts into submission, but it proved so unwieldy it was scrapped. On another occasion the Angrians seized tons of arms and ammunition and Bombay's annual supply of gold.

Not until the 1750s, when William James commanded the Company's Angrian campaign, did technological supremacy bring the British victory.

SIR WILLIAM JAMES
In his youth, William James (1721-83) ran away to sea to avoid being punished for poaching. Toughened by experience, in 1751 he was made commander of the East India Company's Bombay navy. Within five years he had destroyed the Angrian pirate fleet.

PIECES OF EIGHT

PIECES OF EIGHT Pieces of eight, (*above*), the famous Spanish coins from the age of piracy, were worth one silver dollar. They were called pieces of eight because they were worth eight reals, and a real was one eighth of a dollar. Pirates were very careful about sharing their plunder equally (*below*), partly because they usually made agreements before going into action, and partly because swindlers soon came to a nasty end!

GUNFIGHT AT SEVERNDROOG

In 1755 James felt strong enough to tackle the forces of Angria head on. He decided to concentrate his attack on their base at Severndroog. While soldiers attacked from the land, he moved in with his ships. To begin with, it looked as if the venture would fail. But James urged the *Protector* so close to the fort defending the harbour that it was unable to bring its guns to bear on the ship. After a massive gunfight, the fort blew up when the ship hit its magazine (*above*).

THE PIRATE SCHOONER

Pirates operated in every kind of ship, from galleys to junks. Usually they had no choice – they sailed in whatever vessel they captured. The type of schooner shown here was built from the mid-18th century onward. It was an ideal craft: fast, maneuverable, and with a shallow draft that allowed her to hide in rivers and bays. The sail plan, with square sails only at the tops of the masts, allowed the boat to sail close to the wind. "Schooner" comes from the American verb scoon, meaning to skim along the water.

Note that this ship is not heavily armed. Cannons were expensive to operate, their weight slowed the ship down, and they were only used against unarmed vessels. Besides, no pirate wanted a gunfight. They aimed to strike fast and get away as quickly as possible.

Captain's Cabin
Placed at the stern, this was out of the worst of the weather and could be easily defended in case of mutiny. It was also the store-room for charts and money.

powder · wadding · shot

UNDER FIRE
Cannons (*above*) were loaded through the muzzle with powder, wadding, and shot. A gun's recoil, capable of breaking a man's leg, was absorbed by ropes. A single cannon ball weighed 20 lb (9 kg). To get greater range and hit a vessel on the waterline, gunners skimmed shots off the sea (*below left*). Double balls and shrapnel (*below right and middle*) were used against the rigging to do the most damage.

Sail Locker
A storm could carry away the entire rigging, so all ships carried spare sails. They had to be kept dry to prevent rotting.

Stores and Armory
These were kept at the bottom of the boat due to their weight. To prevent damage they were tied down in rough weather.

*A schooner
with all
sails set*

CHART POWER An accurate chart of a stretch of newly discovered coast could prove more valuable than gold! In 1682, Bartholemew Sharpe and two friends were tried for piracy before the High Court of the Admiralty. Despite having killed 200 people, sinking 25 ships, and doing damage valued at 4 million pieces of eight, all three were found not guilty. The reason – Sharpe had captured a book of charts of the South American coastline. On his return to England he had presented them to King Charles II. The king himself made sure Sharpe came to no harm.

Galley
The galley was the ship's kitchen. Due to the risk of fire, the stove was built of brick and iron, with a bucket of sand always at the ready to put out the fire in rough weather.

Rigging
A ship carried many hundreds of feet of hemp rope, as well as pulleys (blocks), sails, and spars (the beams from which sails were hung). The mainstays (shrouds) of the masts were crossed with ratlines.

Show a Leg!
The hammock was invented by native Caribs and adopted by sailors as a bed on board ship. The phrase "show a leg," meaning "get on with it," was originally a command for sailors to get up out of their hammocks (below).

Windlass
The mainsails and their spars were tremendously heavy, especially when wet. The windlass enabled a few men to raise them quickly. It was also used for lifting the anchor.

Anchor
An absolutely essential piece of equipment used when there was no safe harbor or jetty nearby.

The Toilet!
When pirates wanted to relieve themselves, they went to a rope cage suspended over the sea in the bows.

Ballast
kept the ship upright.

PIRATES OF THE EASTERN SEAS

Local pirates in the Far East stalked the Sea of Japan, the Yellow Sea, and the East and South China Seas. But with the arrival of the Europeans came competition. By the end of the 16th century, the Portuguese had a stranglehold on trade in the Sea of Japan. Then British buccaneers nosed into the warm waters of the Pacific Rim, preying on European and native shipping. By 1800, as China's Qing dynasty went into decline and as the demands of European traders became increasingly harsh, Chinese pirates had grown in strength and numbers. The fleet of Ching Yih (page 42) was powerful enough to ignore the imperial Qing navy. However, with the collapse of Ching's fleet in 1810 and the foundation of European bases at Singapore (1819) and Hong Kong (1841), the great age of Chinese piracy drew to a close.

A Boatload of P...

B ETTER DEAD THAN ALIVE! The cruelty of Chinese pirates (*above*) toward prisoners was equal to any buccaneer atrocity. Captives were held in cramped squalor and fed rats, rice, and caterpillars (*right*). Some reports told of men having their feet nailed to the deck before being beaten to death, and of prisoners being cut up and eaten!

The Junk

Pirates converted cargo junks by adding guns and rowing boats (needed for boarding and making coastal raids). The largest three-masted junks were almost 600 tons. Measuring some 100 ft (30 m) by 20 ft (6 m), they carried 400 men and 30 cannons. Massive oars helped the ship maneuver in tight corners or light winds. Captains lived on board with their families.

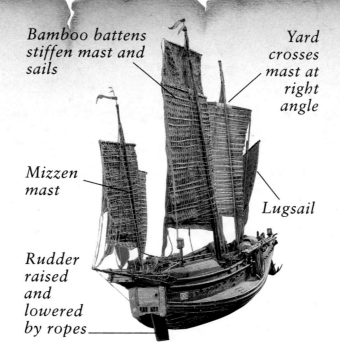

Bamboo battens stiffen mast and sails

Mizzen mast

Rudder raised and lowered by ropes

Yard crosses mast at right angle

Lugsail

ORIENTAL WEAPONS

Pirates of the East were only too pleased to get their hands on Western cannons and muskets, and by the 18th century they were making their own cannons, adapted to their own needs. For example, they liked to have small, swiveling cannons on the bows of their ships. Otherwise, they used a variety of local weapons. As well as carved swords and knives, they used spears, blowpipes, and axes.

Dao sword: *this razor-sharp weapon (below)* was *often decorated with human hair.*

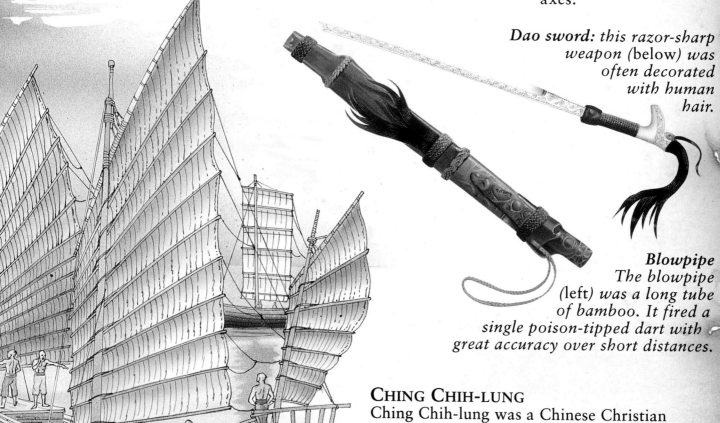

Blowpipe

The blowpipe (left) *was a long tube of bamboo. It fired a single poison-tipped dart with great accuracy over short distances.*

CHING CHIH-LUNG

Ching Chih-lung was a Chinese Christian pirate, also known as Gaspar Nicholas, whose power was second only to that of the Ming emperor. For over 20 years his fleet of 1,000 junks and private army of Dutch and African soldiers enabled him to rule the coast between Guangzhou (Canton) and the Yangtze River like a king. He was ambushed in 1646 and executed in 1661. Power passed to his son Koxinga, but when he died in 1662, the pirate kingdom quickly broke up.

WEST MEETS EAST

The final flourish of Chinese piracy followed the end of the East India Company's monopoly of trade with China in 1838. Merchants of every seafaring European nation headed east. The pirates, of course, were there to meet them. Britain acted swiftly to meet the challenge and by 1849 the last great pirate fleet had been destroyed. At the same time action was being taken against sea robbers (*left*) along the Strait of Malacca and among the countless islands of the East Indies. Here squadrons of galleys and smaller craft had preyed on passing ships for centuries. But these light vessels were no match for the West's heavily gunned steamers, and by 1850 most seaways had been cleared.

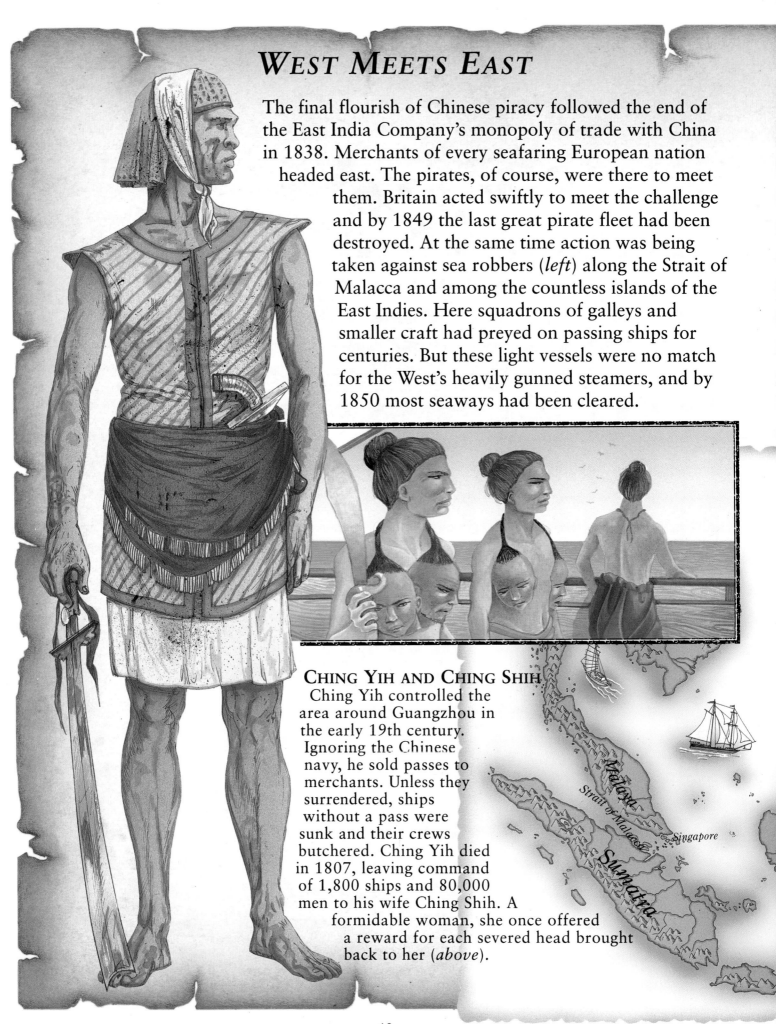

CHING YIH AND CHING SHIH

Ching Yih controlled the area around Guangzhou in the early 19th century. Ignoring the Chinese navy, he sold passes to merchants. Unless they surrendered, ships without a pass were sunk and their crews butchered. Ching Yih died in 1807, leaving command of 1,800 ships and 80,000 men to his wife Ching Shih. A formidable woman, she once offered a reward for each severed head brought back to her (*above*).

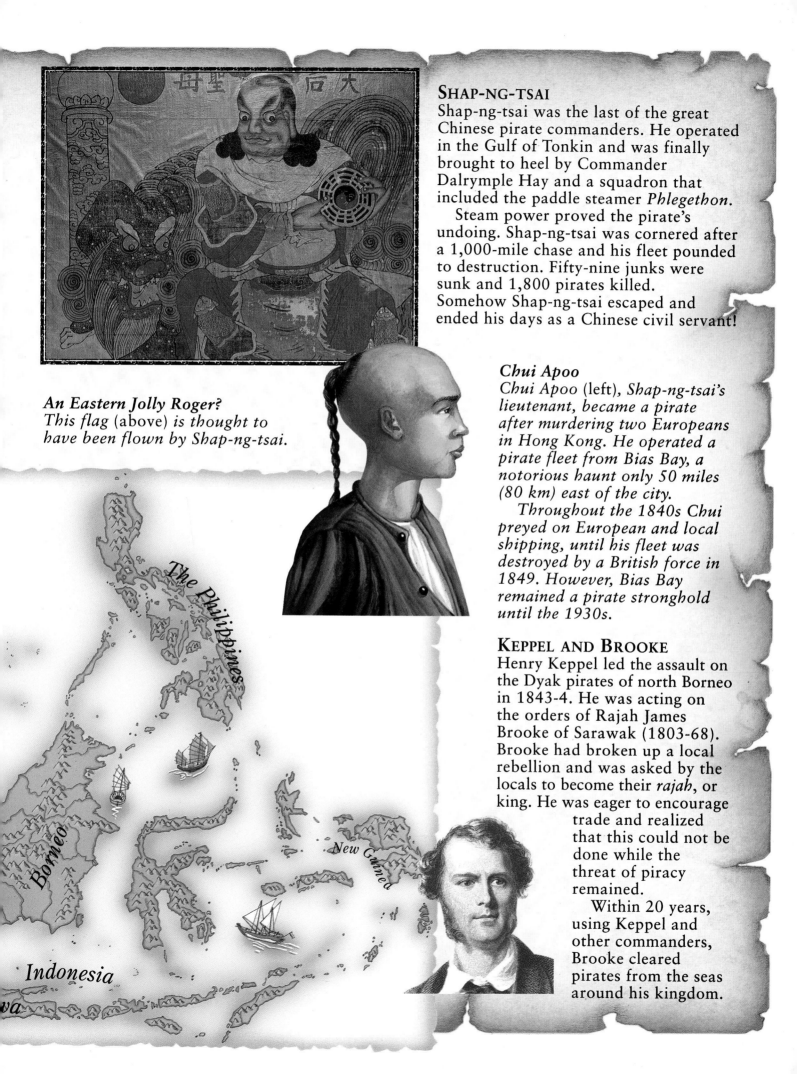

SHAP-NG-TSAI

Shap-ng-tsai was the last of the great Chinese pirate commanders. He operated in the Gulf of Tonkin and was finally brought to heel by Commander Dalrymple Hay and a squadron that included the paddle steamer *Phlegethon*.

Steam power proved the pirate's undoing. Shap-ng-tsai was cornered after a 1,000-mile chase and his fleet pounded to destruction. Fifty-nine junks were sunk and 1,800 pirates killed. Somehow Shap-ng-tsai escaped and ended his days as a Chinese civil servant!

An Eastern Jolly Roger?
This flag (above) is thought to have been flown by Shap-ng-tsai.

Chui Apoo
Chui Apoo (left), Shap-ng-tsai's lieutenant, became a pirate after murdering two Europeans in Hong Kong. He operated a pirate fleet from Bias Bay, a notorious haunt only 50 miles (80 km) east of the city.

Throughout the 1840s Chui preyed on European and local shipping, until his fleet was destroyed by a British force in 1849. However, Bias Bay remained a pirate stronghold until the 1930s.

KEPPEL AND BROOKE
Henry Keppel led the assault on the Dyak pirates of north Borneo in 1843-4. He was acting on the orders of Rajah James Brooke of Sarawak (1803-68). Brooke had broken up a local rebellion and was asked by the locals to become their *rajah*, or king. He was eager to encourage trade and realized that this could not be done while the threat of piracy remained.

Within 20 years, using Keppel and other commanders, Brooke cleared pirates from the seas around his kingdom.

MODERN-DAY PIRATES

With the decline of the British, Dutch and French navies in the second half of the 20th century, in some parts of the world piracy began once more to flourish. Today, attacks on merchant ships in Brazil, West Africa and among the islands of southeast Asia are still alarmingly common.

The smaller the vessel, the more likely it is to be attacked. As in the past, speed is the principal tactic. Pirates roar out from concealed inlets in high-speed power boats and threaten their victim with guns and rockets. Small, valuable objects, such as cigarettes and electrical equipment (TVs, computers, watches), are the favourite loot. The days of the buccaneer may be over, but piracy lives on – in 1991 there were 150 pirate attacks in the waters of Indonesia alone!

THE QUEEN OF THE MACAO PIRATES

Surprisingly, the Chinese tradition of female pirates survived into the 20th century. In the 1920s, when China was torn by civil war, piracy once again flourished on her coasts.

The American journalist Aleko Lilius was sent to investigate the attacks on numerous Western vessels and tracked down Lai Choi San, "the Queen of the Macao Pirates" (*below*). Though a small, innocent-looking woman, her power and fortune were enormous. She made her wealth through raids and ransom-taking. After a series of amazing adventures, Lilius lost track of her and no one knows what eventually became of her. But several rusting hulks along the Chinese seaboard still bear witness to the power of this remarkable woman.

Merchant Targets
Once under way, gigantic modern cargo boats are well-nigh impossible to attack. But at anchor, possibly manned by only a skeleton staff, they make tempting targets (above). The objective of the pirates is to get aboard as swiftly as possible, overpower or avoid the crew, and make off with whatever they can lay their hands on before the alarm is raised.

PIRACY OF PLEASURE CRAFT

Pirates have returned to the Caribbean – their targets are the thousands of yachts cruising around the islands (*right*). The boats alone are sometimes worth millions, and the owners are among some of the richest people in the world. The modern buccaneers like to strike at night, selecting a single craft in an isolated bay and moving in swiftly in high powered boats.

PATROL AND CONTROL

Modern technology has made piracy a more risky business than it was in the past. Most countries have well-equipped naval patrols (*below left and bottom of page*). These are often backed up with aircraft and helicopters, to keep an eye on domestic shipping. And no nation wants a reputation for allowing piracy to flourish in its waters. Ships are in constant contact with the authorities by radio. If they run into trouble, they can pass on their position and call for assistance in seconds. Yet piracy still goes on. Where there is wealth, there will be unscrupulous people trying to seize it. But at least today the pirate's task is rather more difficult than it was in the days of the lumbering treasure galleon.

REFUGEE VICTIMS

One of the most unpleasant forms of modern piracy has been the raids made on boatloads of helpless refugees. Of the hundreds of boats leaving Vietnam in the 1980s, over half were attacked by pirates who robbed "boatpeople" of their last, precious belongings.

NAUTICAL AND PIRATICAL TERMS

Admiralty The office of government (in Britain) responsible for the navy.

Bagnio A prison in Muslim countries where Christian prisoners were held.

Ballast The heavy weight at the bottom of a sailing vessel needed to keep it upright.

Barbary Coast Northwest coast of Africa.

Bilges The area at the bottom of a ship where water collects.

Boatswain (or bosun/bo'sun) The foreman of a ship's crew.

Booty Loot.

Bowsprit The spar projecting from a ship's bow.

Buccaneer A Caribbean pirate.

Careening Scraping marine life from the underneath of a boat.

Chart A mariner's map (see *below*).

Corsair A Mediterranean pirate.

Dhow An Arab-designed sailing vessel with a single triangular sail.

Draught Depth of water a ship takes up.

Dysentery Very serious stomach upset!

East India Company The British company with huge commercial and political power in India from 1600 to 1858.

Galleon A large, three-masted sailing vessel with a high stern.

Galley A ship's kitchen.

Hammock A canvas sling used as a bed.

Hispaniola The original Spanish name for the island which now comprises Haiti and the Dominican Republic.

Jolly Roger The pirate skull and crossbones flag.

Junk A Chinese sailing vessel.

Magazine A gunpowder and armaments store in both forts and ships.

Maroon Abandon, usually in a deserted place.

Merchantman A cargo ship.

Navigation Guiding a vessel across the ocean.

New World The Americas (shown *above*).

Outlaw A criminal living beyond the protection of the law.

Pieces of Eight Gold coins worth a dollar.

Privateer A sea raider operating with his government's permission.

Prize A captured ship.

Prow A ship's bow, or front.

Rais A sea captain in the Muslim world.

Rigging The ropes supporting masts and sails.

Scurvy Disease caused by lack of vitamin C.

Show a Leg Get out of bed – literally to show a leg over the side of a hammock.

Shrapnel Small pieces of metal fired from a gun.

Shrouds Rigging supporting a mast.

Spar A length of wood used to support the sails.

Stem (or stern) The back of a ship.

Tackle Ropes and pulleys.

Trireme A galley built by the Ancient Greeks with oarsmen on three levels (see diagram, *right*).

Windlass A winch used to pull up the anchor.

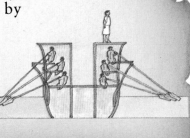

PIRATE TIMELINE

3000 B.C. First ships used by Egyptians for long sea voyages, and start of piracy.

1200-600 B.C. Greek sea raiders dominate the eastern Mediterranean.

400 A.D. Chinese pirate San Wen ravages northern coast of China.

8th to 11th centuries A.D. Vikings spread out from Scandinavia, raiding towns and attacking ships from Iceland to the Black Sea. Arabs conquer the Barbary Coast.

1290 Marco Polo records activities of Gujarati pirates in Indian Ocean.

1492 Columbus discovers America.

1496-1540 Spanish conquest of New World and rivalry with France and Britain leads to huge pirate activity in Caribbean.

1497 Vasco da Gama opens sea route to India and China.

16th-17th centuries Rivalry between Muslim and Christian corsairs in the Mediterranean at its peak.

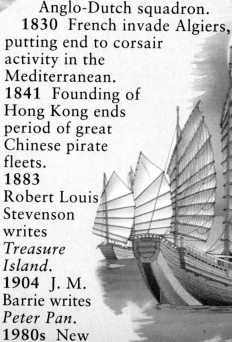

1560 Dragut Reis defeats Spanish fleet.

1562-1585 Francis Drake and John Hawkins carry out a number of daring attacks on the Spanish Main.

1620s Muslim corsairs begin to sail in European galleons as well as in galleys. They raid targets as far away as Iceland.

1627-1646 Ching Chih-lung terrorizes Chinese coast from Yangtze to Canton.

1630-1654 Spanish troops clear buccaneers from Hispaniola.

1655-1680 British governors of Jamaica encourage buccaneers to base themselves in Port Royal.

1660s-1670s Buccaneers drawn in huge numbers from Caribbean to Indian Ocean.

1670 Heyday of the buccaneers – Henry Morgan calls on 1,800 of them in his attack on Spanish Panama City.

1678 Alexander Exquemelin writes *The Buccaneers of America*.

1690-1720 Madagascar main base of European pirates in Indian Ocean.

1690-1729 Kanhoji Angria builds up fleet. Maratha Wars begin.

1692 Port Royal is devastated by a massive earthquake. 2,000 people die.

1718 Maynard hunts Blackbeard down and kills him.

1719 Defoe writes *Robinson Crusoe*.

1720 Mary Read, Anne Bonny, and Calico Jack are captured off Jamaica.

1724 *A General History of the Robberies and Murders of the Most Notorious Pirates* is written.

1755 William James destroys Severndroog and Geriah forts, ending Maratha Wars.

1800s Ching Yih and Ching Shih control fleet of 1,800 junks and 80,000 pirates.

1816 Bombardment of Algiers, by Anglo-Dutch squadron.

1830 French invade Algiers, putting end to corsair activity in the Mediterranean.

1841 Founding of Hong Kong ends period of great Chinese pirate fleets.

1883 Robert Louis Stevenson writes *Treasure Island*.

1904 J. M. Barrie writes *Peter Pan*.

1980s New wave of piracy.

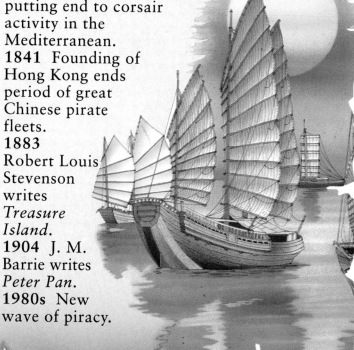

INDEX

Photocredits Unless otherwise stated all pictures in this book were supplied by the National Maritime Museum, London, and we gratefully acknowledge their assistance. The publishers are also grateful to the following for their permission to reproduce pictures and photographs:
(Abbreviations: t – top, m – middle, b – bottom, r – right, l – left) 4-5, 7, 12m, 17b, 18 both, 19, 32, 34m: Hulton Deutsch Collection; 6m: United Artists (Courtesy Kobal); 6b: Warner Bros (Courtesy Kobal); 8, 11t, 13, 15t, 17t, 21, 27t, 35 both, 43b: Mary Evans Picture Library; 11m, 47t: Solution Pictures; 12b: © John Ryan (from the book *Captain Pugwash, a Pirate Story*); 22b: Poseidon Pictures; 24t, 45m & b: Frank Spooner Pictures; 24b: Theatre Projects Films (Courtesy Kobal); 33, 36-37: Delaware Art Museum, Howard Pyle Collection; 45 Spectrum Colour Library.